EARLY WELSH SAINTS

Early Welsh Saints

Daniel J. Mullins

First published in Welsh, St David's Day, 2002
Translated and published in English, 2003

© Text: Author

Copyright © by Gwasg Carreg Gwalch 2002.
All rights reserved. No part of this publication may be reproduced
or transmitted, in any form or by any means, without permission.

ISBN: 0-86381-800-5

Cover picture: courtesy of Henry Jones-Davies, Cambria
Cover design: Sian Parri
Pictures inside courtesy of Terrence and Heather James; C.V. Morgan.

Published by
Gwasg Carreg Gwalch,
12 Iard yr Orsaf, Llanrwst,
Wales LL26 0EH
☎ 01492 642031   ▤ 01492 641502
✆ books@carreg-gwalch.co.uk
Internet: www.carreg-gwalch.co.uk

*Translated from Welsh
by Harri Pritchard Jones*

Contents

Foreword 8

Preface.. 9

Growth of Monasticism.. 10

Continuation of the Christian Faith in Britain.............................13

Teacher of the Saints 16

The Patron Saint of Wales 19

Manipulating the Traditions of a Saint..22

The Lives of the Saints..24

A Short Calendar...27

Bibliography...67

Foreword

The reader will see how much I owe to scholars and researchers, young and old, in the fields of our literature, our manuscripts and all our ancient texts. The first fathers of the Christian Church in Britain wrote in Latin; their training and learning was based on the education in the Roman schools.

At the request of the late John Owen Huws, I set out to write this book. Both of us had been in Ireland preparing a radio programme about the Great Famine. I recall him standing on a hillock in County Limerick looking at the ruins of the cottages of the poor creatures who had to watch ships taking wheat out of the country; staring then at the ridges which are still there today because the potatoes which could have sustained the people had rotted in the ground. Recalling this tragic period led to a discussion about the relationship between Wales and Ireland. In both countries place-names and places the people call holy treasure the memory of the Brython (Briton), Patrick, and the religious heritage that had at one time created a single religious commonwealth, and the early saints of the two islands who felt utterly at home in all parts of it.

It is a cause of great sadness to me that John's untimely death has robbed Wales of one of her most faithful sons, who wished to see his compatriots embracing their own history. In spite of all the faults and weaknesses of this little volume, John was very anxious for it to be published. I hope it is a fitting memorial to him.

Amongst the mess of materialism and the ruins of religion in our day, the testimony of Illtud, Dewi (David) and Deiniol remains, continuing their call to us over the centuries. They were witnesses to a Christian renewal which united Europe and parts of Africa and Asia under the standard of Christ. By recalling their hopes and triumphs we can see Christ's prayer coming to fruition – 'that they may all be one'.

Bishop Daniel J. Mullins

Preface

Just before you reach Fishguard harbour there is a signpost inviting native and visitor to follow the 'Saints and Stones Tour'. Probably most people going for the ferry pass by without noticing the invitation. As a substantial number of them are of Irish extraction, it would be salutary for them to return one day to follow the track which would connect them with their ancestors and their Christian roots.

Since the dawn of history, the ports of Pembrokeshire and west Wales have been means of connecting the inhabitants of the two islands. It was on the campaign trail of some Irish prince that Patrick, a lad of patrician lineage, was captured and taken to Ireland to be sold into slavery. That was how the whole future of the Emerald Isle and its unique contribution to Western civilisation and human history was decided. The ways of Providence are strange, indeed.

What is envisaged here is a journey from Llanwnda to Saint David's. It is certain that the pilgrims of yesteryear who travelled to visit St. David's grave and monastery in Menevia would have visited these churches. In the early period, in this area as elsewhere in Wales, these would have been buildings of wood and plaster. Later, the people built simple but strong churches, extending them as time went on, especially in the Norman period. In many remote places such as these in Pembrokeshire, the place of worship would have been a hermit's cell. The important contribution of the Celtic monks to the Christian world was their evangelising work in the countryside and outside the urban Roman centres. Though the aim of the hermit was to give up everything in order to follow Christ, it was also his duty to lead people to Christ. It was this that led so many Irish monks to travel the length and breadth of Europe - even to the borders of Russia, or to settle in the mountains of Switzerland and Italy. In this respect the Welsh monasteries were different. The complaint of the Venerable Bede, which is echoed in Patrick's Confession, was that the Britons were lacking in missionary zeal.

As we follow the track of these ancient churches today, we are reminded of what has taken place over the centuries. The Normans changed the patron saint of some churches, re-dedicating them to other saints. The most noteworthy example of this was the re-dedication of the Cathedral of Menevia to the Apostle Andrew. And yet, the memory of the old native saints has remained in spite of this, and in spite of all the derision poured on the veneration of saints which was so marked in the enthusiastic early days of the Protestant Reformation. In the folk memory of the people and in their folklore the names of many hermits and humble servants of Christ lived on, testifying to their influence on the life and consciousness of the Welsh through the centuries.

The Growth of Monasticism

According to the Lord himself, those who wish to be disciples of his must deny themselves and take up their cross daily and follow him. (Luke, 9,23). In the Book of Acts, we see the first Christians trying to follow this ideal by selling their property and transferring it to the Apostles. In Acts 21, 8-9, it is said that the four daughters of the deacon Philip were virgins and prophetesses in Cesarea. This story is interesting and significant. Whatever may be the precise significance of the Greek word parthenoi in the Acts, groups of Christian virgins began to form very early in the history of the Church. St Ignatius of Antioch (c.35-c.107) regards such groups of virgins as an important part of the Christian community. The history of the Church has always been written mainly by men, and yet, as we review references here and there, it becomes obvious that the earliest forms of consecrated life were developed amongst women.

In the history of the man who is considered the father of monasticism, Anthony of Egypt, it was the existence of a community of consecrated women which enabled him to make provision for his sister and become a hermit in the desert. The main source of knowledge about Anthony's history is the life of him written by Athanasius, bishop of Alexandria. Anthony was born in Egypt about the middle of the third century and, following the death of his parents, he put his sister in the care of a convent of dedicated virgins and became a hermit. In 285, he retreated into the mountains of the wilderness and lived in an old fort in a remote and wild place called Pispir. Early in the fourth century a number of hermits joined him there, wishing to be disciples of his. His decision to agree to their request was one of the fateful turning points in the growth and development of the Christian Church. In his old age, he travelled to Alexandria to pay his respects to Athanasius, the bishop of that city, and support him his battle against the Aryans. Anthony died a very old man, over a hundred years old, in 356.

A contemporary of Anthony's in Egypt was Pachomius. Like his more famous compatriot, he also was a hermit and the leader and counsellor of a group of disciples. In contrast to other spiritual counsellors, Pachomius insisted that his followers accepted his authority over them, living under one roof and adopting a rule for their consecrated lives. Here is the beginning of monasticism in its full meaning. Other groups adopted the order and rule of Pachomius. By the time of his death in 346, nine monasteries of men and two of women regarded Pachomius as their spiritual father. Athanasius was aware of this development and supported it. A Latin translation of the Rule was prepared by Jerome in

In 339, Athanasius had to flee from Alexandria. He spent three years in Rome and periods in other parts of Italy and Trier in Gaul. The two monks Isidor and Ammonius were his companions on his journeys. Isidor became an influential figure in Rome, especially in the circles of senators and nobility of the city and their families. That was how the soil was prepared in Rome and Italy for the new seed in the Church. The names of Eusebius from Vercelli, Jerome and Ambrose of Milan are associated with the spread of the movement in the West.

From the standpoint of the Celtic countries, the most important figure was Martin of Tours. Being the bishop of that city, he set to to build the great monastery of Marmoutier. It was said that there were two thousand monks at his funeral in 397.

Martin had a disciple called Vitricius (c.330-407). He was a former soldier, as was Martin himself, and became a member of the circle of the monk Paulinus of Nola (c.353-431). When Paulinus was elected bishop of that city, he called on his fellow monks to lead a religious renewal in the diocese. About 386, Vitricius too was elected a bishop, in the city of Rouen. Again, it was the monks who were in the vanguard in taking the faith out of the towns to the country people of Normandy and to the poor. In 396 Vitricius came to Britain. His stay here was an important link in the development of monasticism and in the mission of the monasteries on the isle of Britain.

It was another leader of the movement in Gaul, John Cassian, who built the famous monastery in Marseilles, and another, Honoratus, who founded a very influential monastery on the small island of Lerins, near Cannes. If we can accept the traditions recorded by Tirechan and Muirchiu in the second half of the seventh century, Patrick had been with Germanus in Auxerre and been instructed in Lerins before he returned to Ireland as a bishop. Certainly, these references are reminders of the relationship between the monastic movement in Gaul and the same movement in Ireland. Tirechan tells us that Patrick had travelled in Gaul, Italy and islands in the Tyrrehenian Sea. This is not in inconsistent with Patrick's Confession. In it the saint tells us, he escaped from slavery in Ireland and travelled two hundred miles to catch a ship to his own country. He was accepted on sufferance, and brought on the ship for three days before landing and travelling for twenty-eight days through the wilderness. Ryan believes this difficult passage suggests they had landed in France, not Britain, before being captured by plunderers at the end of the twenty-eight days. Patrick succeeded in escaping and found himself at the mercy of the elements in southern Gaul or Italy. After some years spent there, Patrick returned to Britain before being called back to Ireland as missionary for Christ's Gospel. It would have been on the continent that he would have learnt about the new monasticism that was transforming the Christian life of Europe.

Whatever about that, the ecclesiastic order founded by Patrick was based on the leadership and authority of bishops. Tirechan lists forty-two of them, and adds that there were others as well. But in the old documents, there is reference also to monks and consecrated virgins. Patrick himself, in his Confession, mentions the sons and daughters of minor kings in Ireland who had become monks and virgins of Christ. They were, obviously, the crown and glory of all his endeavours in Ireland. But though they were of great importance to him, it is interesting to note how subsidiary these were in the order he imposed on the Church in the new Christian province. Regarding the later developments in Ireland, it was the order which existed in Britain that was reflected in Patrick's Confession. The leading role of the abbots and abbesses was not advanced in Ireland under his leadership.

As we try to decide when the monastic movement reached Britain, the testimony relating to Patrick is crucial. The two genuine documents of his work which have survived, the Confession and the Letter to Coroticus's Soldiers, are the earliest texts of the Christian Church in Britain. By the second half of the fourth century, the main leaders of the Western Church, Ambrose, Augustine, Jerome, Martin and Paulinus had turned to the monastic movement for colleagues and missionaries. If the tradition that claims Patrick was instructed in the monasteries of the continent is true, then their influence came to Ireland directly from France. But the coming of Vitricius to Britain in 396 shows that the connection between the Church in Britain and that in Gaul was close and influential, and the new movements in the Church and experimental methods of evangelising the common people reached here very early. In the lives of the saints are stored the memory of monasteries in Wales before Illtud started his great work in Llanilltud Fawr (Llantwit Major). All the evidence suggests that the first seeds of the monastic movement had started growing in Britain by the beginning of the fifth century.

Continuation of the Christian Faith in Britain

Bishops from Britain were present in the Council of Arles in 314 AD and other church councils during the fourth century. It was during this century that the Church life was organised following the acceptance of Christianity as the faith of the Roman Empire. Constantine acknowledged Christianity in 313 and though he concentrated more on the East, the presence of representatives of the Bishop of Rome and receiving his approval ensured that unity of faith and moral purity were secured across the Western provinces.

By 410-415, the authority of the Empire had ended in Britain but this did not mean that the Roman order, law and civilisation had disappeared. As the legions retreated, leaders were chosen to ensure continuity and stability. The arrival of Cunedda and his sons in north Wales was an example of this, and it is obvious Patrick considered himself a Roman citizen and his father and grandfather were stewards of the Roman order. His letter to Coroticus tells us that he is not writing to his fellow citizens, but to Coroticus himself and his soldiers who have become allies of devils, the Scots, the Picts and the turncoats, and that because they had killed and captured Christians and ridiculed priests who spoke in the name of Patrick himself.

Socii Scottorum atque Pictorum apostatarumque. The tribes were abandoning the Faith, and Christianity was being usurped by pagan tribes from Germany. Scholars today believe that it was mainly in the towns that Christianity was accepted and that its influence was weaker amongst the owners of the luxurious Roman villas and in the countryside. It is certainly true that the cities or towns were the centres of Imperial law and order, and Christianity could not but weave itself into this administrative framework. As urban life began to break down, the whole system, including the public organisation of the Church, must have become a stagnant lake until disturbed once again by the monastic movement and the monks. It was this movement that converted the British tribes and the remnants of Roman civilisation into a new unity, creating the nation and culture of the Britanni or Britons. It was the heritage held by our early saints, and all this exciting activity that ensured that the ideal of this special people since then has been the Christian religion with the Welsh language.

Sometimes it is said that Christianity waned between the fourth and sixth centuries. The growth of the Pelagian heresy was testimony to the enthusiastic debate about the elements of the Faith on the European continent, and, in turn, Germanus came here in 429 to rid the country of this erroneous interpretation. Patrick testifies to the eminence and importance of the church schools and the churchmen who spent their lives perfecting their learning, rhetoric and knowledge of the Scriptures.

The great contribution of the wandering monks on the continent was taking the Faith out of the town. In Wales, where there were but two Roman towns, the nature and location of the early *llannau* (churches or religious settlements) demonstrates that the monastic missions went through the countryside, and that what was set up there was the monastic form of pastoral care.

A somewhat nebulous figure in the period between Patrick's time and the establishment of Illtud's celebrated school was Dyfrig. He was certainly an historical character and his contribution to the continuation of church life and order was crucial.

There is testimony that Christianity survived in unbroken continuity in Caer-went and the south-east, and that the traditions associated with Macsen Wledig (Maximus Magnus) suggest there were campaigns to secure Christian orthodoxy in those parts. The Roman roads connected the old headquarters of the army with the Towy valley in the south and Anglesey and Gwynedd in the north, the areas Cunedda and his sons were defending. If it is reasonable to date the birth of Gildas at about 500, the education he received in his youth must have been a classical and very Christian one.

The earliest reference to Dyfrig is in the life of Samson. We are told he came to Illtud's monastery to ordain Samson as a deacon and to ordain two others to the priesthood. We are also told it was Dyfrig who ordained Samson as priest and that he lived in 'his own house' on Caldey Island. In the same life we are told of a synod when three bishops were consecrated on the Feast of Peter the Apostle's Chair, on February 22, Samson being one of them.

Once the persecution of Christians had ended, councils came together to establish order in matters of doctrine and discipline in the Church. One of the earliest councils we know of, and of which there are written records still extant, was that of Elvira, in Spain, about 306.

Bishops from Britain assembled in councils during the fourth century. It is quite probable that British bishops summoned a synod or a council in order to secure and rejuvenate the life of the Church. The chief purpose of local synods and councils in the Western tradition was to make certain that the doctrines of General Councils and the ancient traditions of the Church became a part of everyday life across the Christian world. This is true of synods and councils to this day.

The Book of Llandaff claims authority over the churches of Dyfrig, many of them in the diocese of Hereford, and over the churches of Teilo, many of which were in the Menevia diocese (St. David's). On the other hand, as we read the *Vita* and the early lives of the saints which refer to Dyfrig, it is fair to assume that he belonged to a generation of churchmen which predated the days of Illtud. It is mentioned that Dyfrig was consecrated a bishop by Germanus but that is very doubtful. It could be a reference to the re-structuring that came in the wake of the visit of the saint from Auxerre to Britain. Dyfrig belonged to the orthodox tradition of Germanus and the churches in Gaul.

By the middle of the sixth century, the period of peace which followed the battle of Mons Badonicus had ended. The English were pushing on to the west and the north with Roman Britain now confined to this side of the Severn Sea, along the western seaboard and southern Scotland. The churches of Dyfrig were located in the provinces of Ewyas and Archenfield. The first half of the century was a period of waning in religion according to Gildas, and the traditions about Dyfrig suggest that this was true. Mention is made of him consecrating bishops in the South, and consecrating Deiniol and appointing him Bishop of Bangor. All this suggests that he was the link between the remnants of Christianity of the Roman period and the new movement to which all the saints of the sixth century belong. If so, Dyfrig belongs to the second half of the fifth century and the opening years of the sixth, and the patrimony of culture, religion and learning from the Empire had persisted.

Teacher of the Saints

By the sixth century monasticism had reached Wales, establishing itself as a power in the life of the Church. Tathan had arrived from Ireland and established a noviciate for monks in Caer-went. The testimony of Gildas reproaches Maelgwn Gwynedd for retreating from a life of praising God and becoming a plunderer of the Church. Gildas adds that this has happened in spite of his having a teacher who was 'the eloquent teacher of almost the whole of Britain'. As was his wont, Gildas doesn't name the famous man but historians are unanimous that it was Illtud. Remembering that Maelgwn Gwynedd died in 547, one can estimate fairly confidently that Illtud was born sometime during the second half of the previous century.

In a document written in Dol, Brittany, about 610, namely the *Vita Samsonis*, there are the earliest details recorded about Illtud. It is said that Samson's parents took their child to the school of a famous teacher of the Britons, a man called 'Eltut'. Like Gildas, the author of the *Vita* considers Illtud to be the famous teacher of all Britain and the Britons. This testifies to the crucial role of Illtud in the development of the educational and ecclesiastic system, which led to the renaissance in Wales in the sixth century. The *Vita* testifies that this Eltut was a disciple of Germanus and that he had ordained him a priest. In the Welsh lives there is confusion between Germanus of Auxerre and his namesake from Paris, yet there is no doubting the reference here is to the famous defender of the Faith and the leader of the faithful Christians in the battle of the Halleluia.

The author of the *Vita* says that Eltut 'was the most learned of all the Britons, in his knowledge of the Scripture, the Old Testament and the New testament, and in all branched of philosophy - poetry, rhetoric, grammar and arithmetic'. Illtud had received an education in the tradition of the Imperial schools.

The system of the *trivium* and the *quadrivium* was still the foundation of the work of the schools, and one that would remain pre-eminent up to the fourth Lateran Council in 1215, and afterwards. The *Vita* mentions, also, the death Eltut, a history given 'by the Catholic brothers in that place', namely in the monastery of Llanilltud Fawr (Llantwit Major). The tradition that existed in the seventh century, therefore, was that Illtud died in the great monastery. Later certain other churches, which bore his name, would also claim that privilege.

In the *Historia Brittonum* attributed to Nennius, a work that belongs to the eighth century, there is a story of an occasion when Illtud decided to build a church in Oystermouth. By then, therefore, Illtud's monastery had a foothold in Gower. An anonymous bishop or priest was buried there and great honour was given there to Illtud. According to the story some leader *(regulus)* had proved the veracity of dragging a stick around the miraculous altar. This is a reference to the ancient primitive custom that survived in the East and the West, in the religion of Islam as in Christianity, namely the habit of swearing an oath on the grave of a prophet or holy man. In the Middle Ages, oaths were sworn ritually on the graves of Teilo in Llandaff. As the verdict of courts and the claim to land and property especially depended on the veracity of witnesses and testimony, the sanctity of oaths became essential.

In the twelfth century, clerks in Llantwit Major composed the life of Illtud. By then the Normans were an influence in south Wales, and in their opinion the state of the church was scandalous. The old habit of transferring the property of the old monasteries to laymen was completely unacceptable. The Welsh cloister was demolished and though they kept the name, it was regular canons rather than laity who ruled and administered the lands and life of the monastery. Illtud's monastery was converted into a collegiate church, which meant an important church under the governance of a chapter of canons For these clergy, the historical claim of the monastery or church to its lands and property was very important. It is hardly surprising then that the Norman canons collected the local people's stories and folk-memories about the saints of the sixth century. A noteworthy example of this development is the document *Braint Teilo,* Teilo's Privilege, in the Book of Llandaff, and the life of that saint, which prove that there were innate rights pertaining to the bishop of Llandaff. By the end of the twelfth century, the lives of the Welsh saints had been collected, probably in Brecon priory. A similar composition is the *Vita Santi Iltutis Abbatis,* which is a patchwork of tales and legends about Llantwit Major. In contrast to other lives, the author does not claim charters for the monastery. Accepting the testimony of the life, Llantwit Major was by then under the patronage of the Normans. In chapter 26 we are given the story of a raid 'by the men of the north', when 'Robert FitzHaimon ruled Glamorgan'. By then, though its antiquity as a monastic site was of great importance, Llantwit was safe under the patronage of the bishop and the Norman princes of Glamorgan.

According to this life, Illtud was a man of royal lineage. He had been educated in the seven branches of knowledge and art, memorising it all. He also received 'the five keys of knowledge' and he was the most eloquent of all the children of Gaul. He became a soldier and the leader of soldiers. As he was related by blood to King Arthur, he left Brittany and crossed to Britain. He was already married with a virtuous wife named

Trynihid who was his companion on his journeys, and he received the patronage and affection of the king.

Once, out hunting in Glamorgan, the king's soldiers came into Cadog's area. In their arrogance, they sent him a threatening letter. With that power which belonged to many Welsh saints, Cadog made the earth swallow up the soldiers. Illtud was not with them at the time and when he returned, he was stunned at what had happened. Cadog's advice was that he abandon his military career and dedicate his life to serving his Creator. Before he was accepted as a monk by Dyfrig, the bishop of Llandaff, we hear of him leaving his wife. Later in the life, 'the very pure woman' visits the Abbot Illtud. She was now living in the mountains with a love of the Trinity, the love of her life. She built a cell (*habitaculum*) and a bede house to serve the poor and assist widows and nuns.

Wade-Evans dates the life in its present form to about 1140 and the references to Illtud's wife support this. The habit of choosing deacons, priests and bishops from amongst married men was a New Testament tradition (see Tim 3, 1-13) and a condition of their ordination was that they consecrated the rest of their lives to continence. This meant that the man so chosen had to seek the consent of his wife and secure proper arrangements for her for the rest of her days. This custom persisted at least up to the thirteenth century. The ecclesiastic centres for widows and nuns are much older than the abbeys and monasteries. The First Lateran Council in 1123 had confirmed the old discipline. One of the battles the Church had to fight from the outset was to secure that unmarried, celibate clergy was a fact and not just an ideal. The Normans attempted to resurrect this discipline in Wales and Ireland. Monks and monasteries were expected to lead the way as they had professed the three virtues of poverty, purity and obedience.

The lives of the saints reflect the worries and hopes of the period in which they were composed.

The Patron Saint of Wales

Interestingly enough, the first references to the patron saint of Wales are to be found in the Irish Chronicles. Under the events of the year 588, Tirechan mentions *'Dauid Cille Muine'*, referring to his death probably. In the *Chronicles of Inisfallen,* under the year 589, is seen *'Quies Dauid Cille Muine'*. According to Geoffrey of Monmouth:

> That time was two years and forty and five hundred after the birth of the Son of God from the Lady Mary Virgin. And in that time, David blessed archbishop of Caerleon went from this world to rest and to Menevia in a monastery he himself had established where he was buried.

There we have the historic Dewi or David placed side by side with all the legends associated with him.

In the opinion of Sir John Edward Lloyd, David was born about 520. According to the tradition, his father was a prince of Ceredigion (Cardigan) named Sant, and his mother called Non. He was baptised by Aelfyw, bishop of Menevia, but we know very little with certainty about his life. Rhigyfarch wrote his famous life of him during the eleventh century, but the earliest and most important testimony about him is the number of churches dedicated to him, and their location. There are more than fifty of them and all in south Wales. It is significant that there is no ancient church bearing his name in northern Ceredigion.

The opinion of scholars is that the *foederati* that moved to north Wales, namely Cunedda and his sons, had not extended their influence further south than the midlands. The tribe of Deisi from Ireland had created a kingdom in Pembroke since the fourth century. Reading The Life of David and other lives, Christian missionary activity below the River Teifi had to face all the Irish settlements which remained, it seems, pagan. In spite of all the intercourse with the centres of the Irish saints, back home, it had to be acknowledged that not everybody in western Britain considered themselves amongst the godly Romans Patrick mentions. And if N.K.Chadwick is correct in asserting that the Life of Bridget proves that druids were still influential in Ireland during her youth, which was at the end of the fifth century, the pagan Celtic religion had not disappeared completely in David's time.

Everyone who wishes to discuss the historical David must refer to Rhigyfarch's Life of him. The author's intention was to show the antiquity and authority of David's See, namely Menevia. By the time the Normans arrived, the territory and the borders of a bishop were connected with the native kings and princes. It must also be stressed that the consciousness of the nature of the Church and the doctrine that was the basis of all its structure was common to everybody throughout Christendom. The idea that the Church was set apart in Britain before the arrival of the Normans was developed for political reasons in Thomas Cromwell's prefaces to the revolutionary laws of Henry VIII. Uniformity and a Common order throughout the whole Church came about as a result of the Reformation. It was the Roman order which survived in Wales from the Imperial period, even when it was changed on the continent. In as much, the Church in Britain was more conservative and less venturesome than the Church in Ireland.

There is a tradition which predates Rhigyfarch's Life in which David together with Teilo and Padarn are disciples of Illtud, but it should not be assumed that Rhigyfarch and St. David's were unaware of that tradition. The only thing that can be stated for certain is that such a tradition was not relevant nor of any help to anyone who wished to raise the status of the See of Menevia above every other Episcopal see in Wales, and put it on a par with Canterbury itself.

We can discern the influence of Saint David's and the importance of David growing in Wales and beyond it before William the Conqueror sped on a flying visit or pilgrimage to St. David's in 1081. According to the Life of King Alfred, the king called on Asser 'from the extreme west of Wales', and the *Anglo-Saxon Chronicle* mentions the monastery and *parrochia* of David. By then, David's renown had spread to Wessex, and the monastery of Glastonbury claimed it possessed relics of the saint from Menevia. The ancient Welsh poem, *Armes Prydein* (lit. The Prophecy of Britain), which Sir Ifor Williams says must be dated before 937, prophesises that an alliance of the Welsh and the men of Dublin will drive the English out of the Island and they will march to battle under the patronage of David: 'blessed David's standard they will raise'.

In the life, the author chooses those parts of the tradition which show the reticent saint outshining all his contemporaries. When the synod was held at Llanddewibrefi, David stayed in his monastery; according to Rhigyfarch it was Dyfrig and Deiniol who persuaded him to attend. The author's contemporaries believed that the bishops of Llandaff and Bangor realised that the Bishop of Menevia was the wisest and holiest of them all. Also, according to Rhigyfarch, David had spent some time after his ordination with Paulinus, a disciple of Germanus. The author is very careful as he places David in the direct line of those Christian heroes who had secured the survival of the Faith in Britain and the orthodoxy and constancy of its doctrine.

Manipulating the Traditions of a Saint

In Lichfield Cathedral in England is kept the manuscript known as The Book of Chad. It contains the text of the gospels of Mathew and Mark and part of Luke's. It is probable that the copying was done in Ireland, about 700 AD, but it was at one time in one of Teilo's churches in Wales. There are some Welsh glosses in it and margin notes dealing with Welsh matters. It is said the book was offered up to God 'on Teilo's altar'. There is also a record of part of an old legal document legislating about the ownership of land, with Teilo as principal witness to the final agreement. Other witnesses are listed and then 'the whole family of Teilo'. These were probably the Abbot-bishop and all the monks of the institution.

We do not know when the manuscript was moved to England but the book must have been in Wales up to the last century of the first millennium, before the Norman invaded Britain and before the lives that were kept in the collection *Cotton Vesp A xiv* in the British Museum were composed. The Book of Chad does not offer any information about Teilo but it notes that there is an important monastery in Wales and a territorial bishop who claims the name of the saint. The monastic church contains the altar of Teilo, and his family are the residents, under the leadership of the bishop of Teilo'r *parrochia*.

A bishop's authority and the territory of his see would vary according to the fortunes of the local king who gave his patronage to the church and defended it. When Caradog was killed in 1081 as he campaigned to extend his territory to the West, the Conqueror came to south Wales immediately and across to St. David's. From then on the influence of the Norman lords would be important in every aspect of Welsh life and that of the Church. Urban (1107-1139) was the first to call himself the Bishop of Llandaff, and that in a document he sent to Pope Callixtus II in 1119. Before that he called himself the Bishop of Glamorgan. But all his forerunners were 'Teilo's bishops'. His principal monastery was Llandeilo Fawr and it was there he was buried. It was Bishop Joseph, who died in 1045, who moved to live in Llandaff and concentrated his pastoral work on the cloister and church there.

When Urban came into office, his ambition was to extend the territories of his diocese to the west and the east, and ensure that everybody recognised the importance of Llandaff within Wales. In order to do this the bishop and his colleagues set to to collect the old documents, adding to them and making emendations so as to further his own aims and ambitions. Urban had been consecrated in Canterbury by Anselm in 1107. Little was heard of him for twelve years – the period of all the collecting and the ordering of the documents which were put together under the title of The Book of Llandaff. In that book, and as an essential part of it, there is the Life of Teilo, a long, laborious composition. Using old documents, oral traditions and the lives of other saints, it 'proves' the claim of Llandaff on territories and parishes from Cydweli in the west to Ewyas and Archenfield in the Hereford diocese.

Bearing in mind the purpose of the Book of Llandaff, we must be very careful in trying to interpret the Life of Teilo. We are told that Teilo learnt the Scriptures at the feet of Dyfrig as a child, and that he and Samson were disciples of the old hero. According to the Life, it was Dyfrig who discovered the pupil's talent, judging him to be his own peer and deciding that Teilo should succeed him in his school *(magisterium)*. Another tradition claimed that Teilo was a pupil of Paulinus Aurelius, and the Book of Llandaff conflates the two claims.

The relationship between Teilo and David is extremely interesting. Rhigyfarch was just as bent on proving the pre-eminence of St. David's, in the face of the claims of Llandaff, and that David excelled all other contemporaries. In the *Vita*, it is noted that David was a pupil of Paulinus and Teilo one of David's three faithful disciples. According to the Book of Llandaff, it was after he had been a pupil under Dyfrig and Paulinus that Teilo went to stay with David in Carmarthenshire and Menevia. Teilo had already been with David when he stayed with Paulinus, and he and David were of one mind in all matters, wishing for the same things and rejecting the same things also.

In the Life of Teilo we are told that Teilo retreated to 'distant parts' because of the yellow plague. We know Maelgwn Gwynedd had died of this plague and that the pestilence had persisted in the land between 547 and 550 AD. According to the Life of Illtud, it was to Brittany that Teilo had gone.

As far as we can see today, David and Teilo were historical saints from the sixth century and were contemporaries. The lives retain genuine traditions about them. However, the difficulty and the challenge for us is to reach behind the traditions about them and the very practical considerations of the authors, in order to discover the men of flesh and blood who were so important in the formation of our nation.

The Lives of the Saints

The precedents of the lives of saints in every country were the readings which were prepared from the earliest days to be read in the service of Matins. This is part of the public worship of the Church and its aim the praise of God, not to laud individuals. The purpose of the readings is to praise God in his saints and reveal his grace at work in the world and in his servants. The aim is to put before the listener an ideal of life in Christ, rather than offering a factual description of the life of any mortal person. One aspect of this tradition amongst Christians is that of praise found in Welsh literature.

The *Vita* was a literary form that was developed in Latin on the pattern of the classical tradition of recounting and listing the virtues of the gods. Every nation on earth has treasured and passed on the memory of the feats and achievements of its heroes. Within Christian communities, it was a completely natural thing for this custom to lead to ways of commemorating the heroes of the Faith. In addition to Mary and the apostles, honour was paid to special missionaries, the founders of local churches and martyrs by dedicating churches to them and keeping their names in the chapels and churches which kept the relics of the saints. Traditions about them were kept alive in the memory of people in their literature, be it oral or written. It should be noted, also, that the cult of a saint was often used to oust and replace pagan beliefs and habits, and stories which had been told previously about gods and giants were attributed to the Christian hero.

Lives of saints were written in Brittany from the seventh century onwards and there are examples from Ireland from the same period. In the following century the custom started in England. The liturgical readings were much older than these.

According to the Catholic doctrine, the totality of the Church of Christ is present wherever there is a bishop and a community of people under his care. During the tempestuous times which followed the fall of the Empire and its order, cities and towns were left without any system of administering law or of keeping social life in order. The only public figure who was respected and had the trust of the people was the bishop. In those countries that had no Roman order, abbots and abbesses became leaders of communities, in material as well as spiritual terms. Gregory the Great (540-604), the Pope who sent Augustine to England, wrote:

> I am forced to consider questions pertaining to churches and monasteries. Often, I have to be judge of the lives and doings of 'individuals. At one time, I have had to accept a role in civic matters;

then, I worry because of the raids of the barbarians, fearing the lions which are threatening the flock which was given into my care. I have to accept the political responsibility in order to support those who are maintaining the legal order. I have to put up patiently with the horrible misdeeds of robbers and then resist them, and that in the spirit of love.

During a sermon on the verse from Mathew's Gospel, 9, 37, the Pope regretted that the world was full of priests but that only very few of them were doing their proper work in the Lord's harvest. The spiritual world of the Church and the responsibilities of the secular world are all mixed up. This is reflected in the stormy history of the Church and in the lives of the saints.

In the Celtic countries, the monastery became the centre and the focus of the life of the Christian communities. In Wales, as the bishop maintained his importance and influence – administratively as well as sacramentally – the memory of abbots remained, and especially of the abbot-bishops as defenders and leaders of the people. As public cults grew about the saints, virtues and powers were attributed to them which belonged to patriarchs and prophets of the Old Testament and to the apostles and their fellow workers in the New Testament.

The texts of the Welsh lives nearly all belong to the twelfth century. It is certainly true that the versions which we have today are based on older texts and traditions, but they were composed for their time. Most of them can be seen in the manuscript known as *Cotton Vespasian A xiv* in the British Museum. The contents of the manuscript were printed in 1944 in the volume edited for the University of Wales Press by the Reverend Wade-Evans, *Vitae Sanctorum Britanniae et Genealogiae*. It is believed that the Lives were collected probably in Brecon, and that about 1200, though some argue that they were collected in Monmouth. The Normans had already become a power in the principalities and dioceses of Wales. One of the central aims of all the flurry of activity in Brecon was to prove the antiquity of churches and their right to their territories. Since the Westminster Agreement in 1107, a bishop had to pay homage to his Lord for the temporal property of the diocese.

In the Book of Llandaff there are various lives as well as many old documents which came into the possession of the bishop over the centuries, and which were kept in the church in Llandaff and other places. These were all organised in order during the years from the consecration of Urban as bishop by Anselm in 1107 and the start of his big campaign in 1119 to promote his diocese above all others in Wales.

The nature of the kingships and the system of inheritance in the Laws of Hywel the Good had created a confused situation for the Church in Wales. In the beginning, the dioceses and the authority of bishops were organised on monastic lines. Sometime during the Dark Ages, gradually and fairly early, the authority and freedom of a bishop came under the control of the local king. When Herwald, Urban's predecessor, was appointed Teilo's bishop in 1056, it was recorded that he had been elected by the clerics of Glamorgan under the patronage of the king of Glamorgan and his overlord, namely Gruffudd ap Llywelyn of Gwynedd. Glamorgan had been without a bishop since the death of Joseph in Rome in 1045. This uncertainty about how a bishop was elected and the fact that the borders of a kingdom and the effective authority of a bishop could change was a cause of concern in the church, and unacceptable to Anselm and other reformers. And it was not just in Wales that difficulty was encountered in appointing bishops. The see of Canterbury itself had been vacant for four years before Anselm was chosen as archbishop.

The whole matter of the right of kings to appoint bishops became a matter of public argument during the last quarter of the eleventh century, namely what historians call the Investiture Controversy. The meaning of investiture was the right of kings to give the bishop his ring and crozier, the external signs of his office and authority. In England, Anselm was in the middle of the battle between the Pope in Rome and the Emperor, and between the Pope and the Norman kings of England and the king of France. In 1100, Anselm refused to pay homage to the king. A form of agreement was reached in 1122. Though the Papacy had won the battle, kings and princes still interfered in the choice of bishops. From the Welsh standpoint and the Lives, the location and the voice of archbishops became crucial in this choice.

This is the background of the lives we possess today. Henceforth, there was an importance attached to Saint David's and Llandaff, not only to their churchmen but also to the lords and kings of Wales. The ownership of the church lands and their privileges were important, as well as being able to show their independence from the will of the contemporary king, and it was just as important against the assertions and arrogance of the Norman lords and native princes. These considerations were of the greatest importance in the South (*Deheubarth*) which had become, by the twelfth century, so vulnerable to Norman influence, but not only in Glamorgan and the South. There are lives of saints from Powys and Gwynedd in *Vest A xiv* as well.

A Short Calendar

JANUARY

13   Kentigarn – Bishop, Confessor

A contemporary of Colm Cille (Columba) from Iona in the sixth century. The lives say he visited David in his monastery in Menevia when he fled to Wales because of the hostility of Morcant in Strathclyde. He is associated with St. Asaph and is named as Asaph's teacher. His name persists in Llangyndeyrn in Carmarthenshire. He is the patron saint of the archdiocese of Glasgow.

24   Cadog – Abbot, Bishop, Martyr

According to the genealogy, his father was Gwynllyw son of Glywysing (Glamorgan, more or less), and Gwladus daughter of Brychan his mother. He is famous for his learning and wisdom, and the life tells us he moved to Benevento in Italy in his old age and changed his name to Sofias. This is an obvious reference to the fame and influence of the abbey of Santa Sophia which had grown, by the time the life was written, to be a centre of European importance.

His most important monastery was Llancarfan, and a number of churches were dedicated to him in Glamorgan and Gwent. He was killed by the English.

Cadog was one of the pioneers of the monastic movement in Britain.

25   Dwynwen – Virgin

One of Brychan's daughters. She went to the Isle of Anglesey with her sister Ceinwen and they built cells close to each other. Dwynwen is the patron saint of Welsh lovers. Dafydd Llwyd of Fathafarn wrote a poem to her:

> Aeth i Landdwyn at Ddwynwen
> Lawer gŵr o alar Gwen.
> (Many a man went to Llanddwyn
> To Dwynwen in his grief for Gwen.)

25   Gildas – Abbot, Confessor

A monk in the sixth century and author of the famous book, De Excidio et Conquestu Britanniae. The book shows that he received a first class education. Though he was a Briton, or possibly a Pict, he writes from a Roman standpoint. This testifies to the fact that the Roman inheritance was surviving and flourishing amidst the Britons long after the legions had withdrawn from Britain.

The book falls into two sections. The first is a review of the history of Britain during the Roman period and afterwards. The second, which is the major part in its length and size, is a sermon against the sins of the age. Maelgwn Gwynedd (who died of the yellow plague in 547) was still alive and holding court in Deganwy. Gildas is complaining that the morality of the age was deteriorating and that because of too much luxury. He describes a peaceful period.

Gildas says he was born in the same year as the battle of Mons Badonis, which was about 500 AD. According to the lineages, his father was Caw from Pictland. A number of churches were dedicated to him in Brittany and it quite possible that he composed his book in that country. Had he been living amongst the kings of Christian Britain he would hardly have been so bold in his condemnation of them. In one of the lives it is said that he spent seven years on the isles of Flatholm and Steepholm in the Severn Estuary. These islands are associated with the retreat periods of monks preparing for a life of service in the name of Christ.

Gildas died in Brittany.

FEBRUARY

1   Ffraid/Brigid – Virgin, Abbess

The general consensus is that Brigid, one of the three patron saints of Ireland, flourished during the first half of the sixth century. Her life was composed in the seventh century by a monk called Cogitosus. The text of the life was published in *Acta Sanctorum Hiberniae* (Edinburgh, London 1888) and has been much discussed. Though it is such an early work it contains many traditions from the pre-Christian period in Ireland. Obviously, there were pagan remnants and fear of the old Celtic gods were elements which were very resistant to Patrick's homilies and his successor bishops.

From the beginning, the Christian Church had to face customs which were sacred to tribes and peoples. As they came to Christ, the centuries-old customs remained. What was done was to preserve the holy places and feats of the nations and sanctify them by association with the rites and heroes of the Faith. The most obvious example is the Feast of the Nativity.

In Ireland, Brigid's name was associated with Brig, goddess of fire, replacing her name for that of the old goddess. This led to doubts about whether the saint had ever really existed. When the Normans arrived in Ireland they found that a constant flame burned before the shrine of her monastery in Cill Dara (Kildare). This custom persisted up to the Protestant Reformation, and that in spite of an edict against it by the

Archbishop of Dublin in 1220. This is not an example of trying to prove that she was a mythical figure, but rather to show how old customs gathered about a historical character.

In the history of Brigid, the monastery became a centre of the country's spiritual life. As there were no Roman style civil and urban centres in Ireland, it became the custom to use the word *civitas* for the monasteries as they became the centres of the ecclesiastic order, and it was there the bishops officiated. In Ireland, though not in Wales, an abbot, or abbess such as Brigid, remained the head and authority in the civitas. There was a difference between the authority of the ordained order of bishops and that of abbots, something that was alien to every other part of the Christian world which had inherited the law and order of the Empire as basis of their ecclesiastic order.

In Wales, many churches were dedicated to Brigid, though the form of her name varied. The earliest of these churches are in the parts of Britain where immigrants from Ireland had settled in the fifth and sixth centuries. There are churches to Brigid across the Celtic countries. Professor E. G. Bowen notes that the later dedications belong to the period of the Viking raids. He argues that the Welsh were aware that she was not a Welsh saint and that the usage of the word sant (saint) as in Llansantffraid, with the name of the church shows this. There are churches bearing her name throughout Wales, from Englefield to Saint-y-Brid (St. Brides Major) in Glamorgan. .

9   Teilo – Abbot, Bishop, Confessor

Of all the historical saints of the sixth century, the most difficult to discover much about him is Teilo. It is certain that he was a contemporary of Saint David and the two are always associated together with Padarn. These three saints were the leaders of the monastic and missionary movement across the south. Teilo was a disciple in Illtud's monastery and is also associated with Paulinus in Llanddeusant, Carmarthenshire. There is a fairly safe tradition that he also spent some time with David in Menevia. A later story, as far as we can judge, is the one about him and David and Padarn going on a pilgrimage to Jerusalem.

Teilo built his chief site in Llandeilo Fawr and it was there he was buried. Up to the beginning of the twelfth century, the bishops of south-east Wales were known as Teilo's bishops.

The best testimony to Teilo is the churches and chapels which bear his name. These show that he played a part in the effective missionary movement which started in the west and made its way along the old Roman roads to Breconshire and Radnorshire and on to Gwent. Not only were Teilo and David contemporaries, but they were also colleagues in the powerful religious renaissance of their time.

10   Fagan – Bishop, Confessor

According to the medieval legend, Fagan and his colleagues were sent by Pope Eleutherius in the second half of the second century. William of Malmesbury names him and Dyfan in his book on the history of Glastonbury.

Throughout the Middle Ages, there were many attempts to fill the gap in the history of the Christian faith in Britain. Augustine came to the English in 597 but the Church was part of the patrimony of the Britons without a missionary or saint remembered as apostle to them. The names of early and historic Christians were deliberately associated with the legends that were devised. It is quite probable that Fagan was amongst these. His name is preserved in the village near Cardiff as well as in a church in Aberdare.

17   Curig – Confessor

A saint of the sixth century and the patron of Llangurig in Montgomery. His name is also preserved in churches in Carmarthenshire and the Vale of Llugwy in Arfon. In the time of Giraldus Cambrensis his crozier was kept in the church of St.Harmon in Radnorshire.

There are no details of his life extant. Since very early times the Welsh saint was confused with the boy Cyricus who was martyred with his mother during the Diocletian persecutions, a persecution which lasted from 303 till the Edict of Milan in 313. There is a saint called Kirik remembered in Brittany on February 17, but he was probably someone else.

Curig is named twice in the poems attributed to Huw Cae Llwyd in Leslie Harries's volume. The first reference is in the elegy for Dafydd Mathew of Radyr (see page 47). As he grieves for his misfortune in the *Cywydd Merch* (Ode for a Woman), (page 121) the poet says:

> *Didal am dewi ydwyf*
> *Digon dig wrth Gurig wyf,*
> *Gwae a ddywed gweddïau*
> *Ag y sydd wedi'i gasáu!*

> (I'm not willing to shut up
> I'm pretty mad with Curig.
> Woe he who prays
> But is hated.)

MARCH

1 David – Abbot, Bishop, Confessor

We are certain that David lived during the sixth century. The testimony of the Irish sources puts the date of his death as March 1, 589. In the lives of the Irish saints David is associated with the names of Ailbe, Bairre, Declan, Molua, Aidan, Finnian and Senan. With the exception of Finnian and his famous monastery in Clonard, these are saints with their main sites in river valleys. The estuaries of rivers and the fruitful riversides were very important to the inhabitants of Wales and Ireland as they travelled back and forth across the Irish Sea. The small ports and the estuaries of the rivers facilitated the traffic between the two countries for the violent plunderer as well as the pacifistic saints. During the fifth and sixth centuries there were strong Irish influences in Pembrokeshire; the Deisi tribe from the Waterford area had settled there before the birth of David. Declan is the chief saint of that part of Ireland. The same was true about the other saints. The mouths of the Slaney in Loch Garman, the Suir in Waterford, the river Lee in Cork and other rivers in the south and south-east of Ireland were the easy routes for the to-ing and fro-ing which was part of the life and experience of Christians between Patrick's mission and the Viking raids. One should not forget the Shannon either, Ireland's largest river, where Senan built his cell and seminary. If David ever went to Ireland, he would have visited Clonard.

Wales and Ireland were a commonwealth of Christians in the sixth century and the sea was a highway between the monasteries. That is the reason for the choice of site in each case, including David's monastery in Menevia. Its is possible he built his first cell in Henfynyw (Old Menevia) in Ceredigion.

David was born into a community which was heavily influenced by Irish elements. Reading his life and being aware of earlier traditions, it is possible to argue that the Irish tribes in Wales were unchristian and aggressive. The Ogham stones show that there were two languages, Irish or remnants of it and the Brythonic, as well as learned Latin, that was in use in the area. Remembering the period David lived in, Brythoneg must have disintegrated to a great degree by the time of his youth and the new, Welsh, language was beginning to appear. It is impossible to say what David's first language was. All the traditions which connect him with the Irish saints and which connect them with Menevia show that the monks of both islands understood each other. It is certainly true that Latin was the language of the schools, the services and learning of the monasteries but even amongst the saints, easy and free communication was an essential of everyday life.

It was in Illtud's monastery that David received his education and formation as a monk. As he ignores this fact and concentrates on the connection with Paulinus and the centres of learning and religion in Ireland, Rhigyfarch emphasises other aspects on David's development, keeping an eye at the same time on the main message and purpose of his Life.

The testimony of the Penitential Books associated with the name of David say that he was strict in his discipline as compared with his contemporaries. This suggests that the image of monks rejecting the help of animals as they laboured was a genuine one. This is supported by the name *'Dyfrwr'* (Waterman) given to him.

David's main missionary territory was Pembrokeshire, south Ceredigion and Carmarthenshire. Churches were dedicated to him in the Gower, the valleys of the Towy and the Wye, in Radnorshire and west Hereford. David and his disciples travelled along the length of the Bristol Channel and along the old Roman roads as he called the Welsh back to Christ.

Of the earliest Celtic Penitentials, three are thought to be connected with St. David's. It is suggested that the records of sixth century synods, including that of Llanddewibrefi, formed the material for these Penitentials.

2   Non - Widow

David's mother according to tradition. The churches, which bear her name are in the same areas as those dedicated to David, in Ceredigion and Carmarthenshire mainly.

The ruins of Non's chapel and Fountain are above the sea by St. David's, and easily reached from the Pembrokeshire Coastal Path.

11   Paulus Aurelianus – Bishop, Confessor

There are various versions of the name Paul in the Welsh lives and calendars. It is probable that a number of monks had been given or adopted the name of the apostle of the Gentiles, and that a hazy memory of them had persisted. (See November 24, below.)

17   Patrick – Bishop, Confessor

Of all the saints of Britain and the Celtic countries, Patrick is the most famous. As well as the Irishman Columbanus, he is the only one in the calendar of the universal Church, and Columbanus was only given that honour recently.

There are two documents attributed to Patrick and they can readily be accepted as genuine. One of them is a letter to Coroticus, leader of the Britons, and the other is his Confession. It appears that they were

The church of Llangar, near Whitland, Carmarthenshire, showing the remains of earlier digs, possibly prehistoric, around the circular graveyard. (Photo: Terry James, with the permission of Archeologica Cambrensis.)

Llandeilo, showing the possible line of the Roman road.
(Photo: Terry James, with the permission of Archeologica Cambrensis.)

Llangynog church – a classical example of a round graveyard in a llan.
(Photo: Terry James.)

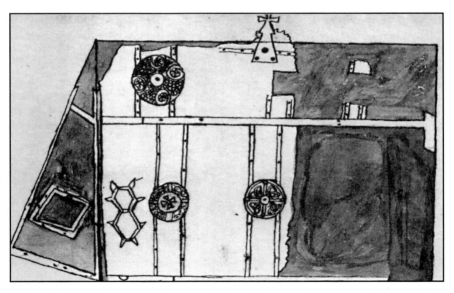

Drawing by Edward Lluyd, or one of his colleagues, of the 'shrine' of Winifred at the end of the seventeenth century. (Photo: Bodleyan Library, Oxford.)

The church of Clynnog Fawr.

The gatehouse of Clynnog Fawr.

The church of Llan-dawg, Carmarthenshire. (Photo: Colin Morris.)

The graves of three pilgrims. (Photo: Colin Morris.)

St David and the dove - a sculpture by John Petts in the Catholic Church in Briton Ferry, Glamorgan.

A statue of St David by St David's Well, Ballinaslaney, Ireland.

Pilgrims: David's Well, in Ballinaslaney, dates back to the seventh century.

St David's cathedral in Glyn Rhosyn.

Non's well, near St David's.

St Brynach's cross, Nevern.

Bardsey Island, sought by pilgrims and graveyard of twenty thousand saints according to tradition.

The church of St Hywyn, Aberdaron.

The church of St Gwynhoedl, Llangwnnadl.

The church of Pistyll, near Nefyn.

The church of St Beuno, Carnguwch.

Lligwy Chapel, an ancient shrine in Anglesey.

The church of St Cwyfan in the west of Anglesey.

The ruins of Dwynwen's church, Llanddwyn.

The church of St Tysilio on an island in the Menai Straits.

Seiriol's Well, Penmon.

An early Celtic cross, Penmon.

A medieval building on Seiriol's island (Puffin Island).

St Trillo's cell, Llandrillo.

A well in the graveyard of the early church of Llangelynnin, high above the Conwy valley.

A low door as entrance to Llanrhychwyn church, above Trefriw.

The porch and a small stone by the church of Caerhun built on an old Roman fort.

Early Christian stones in Penmachno church.

47

Llandanwg church in the dunes of Meirioneth.

The springs of Winifred, Holywell

composed in that order. The one to Coroticus is a letter excommunicating his soldiers. It is quite probable that the Confession was a response to bishops or abbots in Britain who refused to acknowledge Patrick's right to punish Christians outside Ireland. In it Patrick, in the manner of Paul, accepts the criticism of his beraters, that he is lacking in learning and instruction, but he responds forcefully by justifying all his efforts as he was an exile amongst barbarians, whilst his critics stayed at home to perfect their rhetoric and learning. When he calls himself an unlearned countryman, the scorn and the tongue in cheek element in his writing is scathing and biting.

Patrick says he was born in Britain, and that his father and his grand-father were Roman officials. He was born at the end of the fourth century, about the time Maximus had moved the last legion from Britain to the continent. There has been much discussion about exactly where he was born, but it can be said with a fair degree of certainty that it was in Wales.

At sixteen years of age, Patrick was captured and brought to Ireland as a slave 'with thousands of others according to our merits, because we had deserted God and rejected his commandments'. The apathy of youth towards religion is an old experience in the life of the Christian Church. Patrick looked after sheep in the Wood of Fochoill in Ireland for six years. In his loneliness he turned to his God in constant prayer.

After he had escaped he wandered for a while and then, after a few years, 'I was in Britain with my relatives'. There he heard the voice of a man called Victoricius calling him to return and walk again amidst the Irish. In 432 he went to Ireland as a missionary bishop. There were some Christians there already but it cannot be gainsaid that he is the apostle of the island. Tradition records that he died in 461. Recent scholarship favours the year 493.

Patrick names his father as Calpurnius and his grand-father as Potitus. He says his father was a deacon and his grand-father a priest. Muirciu has recorded a tradition that his mother was a sister of Martin of Tours. For him being a Christian was synonymous with being a Roman. According to the tradition, his message to his new converts was 'In so much as you are Christians, be Romans as well.'

29   Gwynllyw – King, Confessor
According to the lives he was a chieftain *(regulus)* of the lands between the rivers Usk and Rhymney. His wife was Gwladus, a daughter of Brychan, and the abbot Cadog was a son of theirs. We know nothing of the life of this local king, but it is said he died in old age and was buried in Newport where the cathedral which bears his name stands today. He belongs to the fifth century, with the few traditions connected with him recalling the

efforts to defend western Britain against the invading tribes from the continent.

If the general consensus about the location of Mons Badonis is true, the frontier between the English tribes and the native Britons was at that time in the Swindon area. There was peace for a while, and according to Gildas, religious deterioration. If the assertions about the period of Gwynllyw are near the truth, he flourished when the battles against the English were at their height.

APRIL

5   Derfel Gadarn – Confessor

The patron saint of Llandderfel according to *Valor Ecclesiasticus,* and there is a chapel dedicated to him in Llantarnam in Gwent. The adjective added to his name (Firm) led Iolo Morgannwg to promote him as a soldier, but the tradition is an old one. In his ode of praise to Hywel ap Dafydd, Lewis Glyn Cothi says:

> *Ban fu a llu yn eu lladd*
> *ar Gamlan wŷr ac ymladd*
> *Derfel o hyd yn ei arfau*
> *A rannai ddur yno'n ddau.*

> (Loud noise and many killed
> in battle on Camlan
> Derfel still in his suit of arms
> Cleaved steel into two.)

The same poet also refers to *Derfel Feudwy* (Derfel the Hermit) (op. cit. p. 26).

In letters to Thomas Cromwell, Elis Prys, Plas Iolyn, asks for guidance about the effigy of Derfel which was much revered in the parish and district of Llandderfel. He was advised to send it to London, and that is what was done in spite of much protesting in the parish. When the Franciscan John Forest was burnt at the stake in May 1583, for refusing to accept the ecclesiastical supremacy of the king in Henry VIII's reign, the effigy of Derfel was used as fuel for the execution.

6   Brychan – King, Confessor

A king of an Irish settlement in that part of Wales which bears his name. The testimony we have shows that Brycheiniog (Breconshire) was very much under Irish influence during the decline of the Empire. Welsh tradition connects all of this with the name of Brychan, king of most of modern Breconshire, apart from Builth. According to the legends, he was son of an Irish king and his mother Marchell was a daughter of a British king. He is said to have had a very large family and the Triads say he had three wives, and his descendants were one of the three holy tribes of the Isle of Britain.

Twelve sons and twelve daughters are listed as children of his and Giraldus Cambrensis claims he had twenty-four daughters. William of Warwick goes further and says he had twelve sons as well. It is not surprising therefore that there exists a Triad naming Brychan amidst the Three Stocks of the Isle of Britain, the children of Brychan of Brycheiniog, those of King Cunedda and the children of Caw from Brydyn (Pictland). The suggestion in the triad is that the three are contemporaries. The grandchildren of Brychan are saints of the sixth century. Therefore Brychan must have been a Christian king of the fifth century. The lineages and the triad maintain the tradition about his period and his importance.

Brychan's children are associated with those places in Wales and Brittany which maintain the traditions about Paulinus. That saint, together with Dyfrig, are the two named as connecting the period of Saint Germanus with and the Age of Saints in the sixth century. Dyfrig's churches are in Archenfield and nearby Breconshire. This all suggests that these areas in south-east Wales were central in the persistence of the Christian faith in this part of the country. Many of the churches in Breconshire bear the names of the sons and daughters of Brychan. There is a strong tradition that he brought up a family of Christians and that they, in turn, and other children from his kingdom, had become missionaries for Christ, not only in Hereford, Glamorgan and Dyfed, but also to Cornwall before the connection between south Wales and the southern side of the Bristol Channel was broken by the English by the end of the sixth century.

All the stories about Brychan that have been preserved are legends, and yet they do keep in memory the remarkable renaissance of religious life in the areas of Breconshire and all of Wales.

14 Caradog – Confessor

We know little of Caradog and there are only a few traditions about him which have survived. Giraldus Cambrensis wrote to Pope Innocent III (who was on his throne from February 1198 till July 1216) asking him to canonise Caradog.

15 Padarn – Abbot, Bishop, Confessor

A contemporary of David's and Teilo's, but possibly older than them. It is said the three of them went on a pilgrimage to Jerusalem and received a personal gift each from the Patriarch there. In a manuscript from the book by Saint Augustine on the Trinity, which is kept in Cambridge, in the hand of Ieuan ap Sulien, which therefore belongs to the end of the eleventh century, there is a verse about a crook, namely a *baculum*, Padarn's crozier. The verse tells us that there is no relic in the whole world which can compare with Cyrwen, remarkable gift, Padarn's episcopal staff. The nature of the gift given him is of some importance according to the tradition, as the bishop's crozier is the sign of his pastoral and spiritual authority.

Padarn's name is associated now with Llanbadarn Fawr near Aberystwyth. He, together with David and Teilo, were the most famous saints of south-west Wales. Padarn's name was preserved as patron of churches in south Ceredigion and also churches in the uplands of Radnorshire on the old Roman road between the fort of Brecon and the north.

E.G. Bowen argued that Padarn was closer to the old order of the final period of the Empire in Britain than David or Teilo. Not only was his name a common Roman one, but also that he came from south-east Wales and his mission depended on the system of roads which was decaying by David's time. This would prove that Padarn was older than the other two, possibly a contemporary of Gildas.

21   Beuno – Abbot, Bishop, Confessor

One of the remarkable facts about the traditions of the saints is that there was nothing comparable to Illtud's school named in north Wales. The memory of the teaching in the schools has not survived there. And yet the Memorial Stone to Cadfan in Llangadwaladr in Anglesey bears features and the style of lettering which belonged to the Court of the Emperor in Constantinople, and to the most famous Irish manuscripts.

Beuno was educated in south-east Wales. It should always be remembered the schools mentioned in the early period were places of formation for clerics and monks. From the south, Beuno returned to Powys and became leader of a missionary movement through Englefield to north-west Wales along the Roman road. The traditions note that Aelhaearn, Lorcan the Irishman, Llwchaearn, Cwyfan, Edern and Twrog were disciples of his. A sign of the success of Beuno's mission was the churches dedicated to these and those to himself in Aberffraw and Trefdraeth in Anglesey, Penmorfa and Botwnnog in Arfon, Llanycil and Gwyddelwern in Meirioneth, and Beriw and Betws Cedewyn in Montgomeryshire. There are more churches dedicated to Beuno in north Wales than any other saint from the early period.

Beuno was famous for his daring in challenging King Cadwallon, and also for cursing Caradog, causing the earth to swallow him, as a punishment for decapitating Winifred, Beuno's niece. Giraldus Cambrensis says that such daring and confidence is noteworthy of the Welsh in their dealings with their princes and chieftains. King Cadwallon can be dated fairly accurately. He was a son of Cadfan from the line of Maelgwn Gwynedd who succeeded his father and reigned in Gwynedd about the year 625. He allied himself with Penda, the king of Mercia and won a famous battle opening Northumberland to his army. But he plundered the country. Oswald fought against him and killed him in a sudden raid in 633. The arrogance and cruelty of Caswallon give significance to the praise given to Beuno's daring.

MAY

12   Asaph – Abbot, Bishop, Confessor
In the old calendars the first of May was kept as Asaph's Feastday, the date he died on. He was a disciple of Cyndeyrn and it was when that saint came to Powys that Asaph took his first steps towards the monasticism of the period. A native of Englefield, the old form of his name was Asa which English lips turned into Asaph.

That form, the usual one today, goes back no further than twelfth century.

A three day fair is held in St. Asaph at the beginning of May. This was a custom across Europe. Often, the fair was held the day after the feastday. but by the time of the Methodist Revival it was mainly the jollity and fun of the fair that remained.

16   Carannog – Bishop, Confessor
Carannog's life is to be found in Cotton Vesp A xiv, and starts by saying that his feast should be kept by everyone who believes in God. It also says that he followed Patrick to Ireland and that they had divided that island into two. According to the life, he was born in Ceredigion in the period when the Irish were attacking Britain. In the second life, it is said he was descended from Cunedda, and that his father's name was Ceredig. He is the saint named in the church of Llangrannog.

21   Collen – Abbot, Confessor
There are only recent copies of his life preserved. It is said he was a son of Gwynedd , whose mother Ethni was Irish and a daughter of Matholwch. Collen is a seventh century saint, and it is said in his life that he vanquished Bras, chief hero of the pagan English, and put an end to the wars between Christians and pagans in Britain.

In a report from 1749, it is said Collen's body rested in 'the Old

Church' in Llangollen. He is patron of churches in Cornwall and Brittany.

22   Elen - Virgin

The Elen Luyddog of Welsh tradition. There has been much confusion between her and Constantine's mother. She was the wife of Magnus Maximus the general who led the last legion from Britain to the continent as he claimed the Imperial throne. He was a soldier from Spain who became the leader of the legion in Britain. The Emperor Gratian was killed in battle in Gaul, and Maximus was now master of Britain, Gaul and Spain. He was supported and blessed by Martin of Tours. Maximus was killed in Aquileia in northern Italy in 388. His wife was said to be from Segontium, the Roman fort in Caernarfon, and she went with her husband to the continent and after his death consecrated her life to prayer and good works.

Maximus is associated with the Orthodox movement which was resisting the teaching of Pelagius (c. 354-418). Because of that he and his wife were considered to be amongst those who defended the true faith in Gaul.

28   Melangell – Virgin, Abbess

In the lineages, Melangell was descended from Magnus Maximus and her mother's name was Ethni the Irishwoman. Melangell had to flee from Ireland to escape being forced to marry. She hid in a cave in the hills of Pennant in Montgomeryshire. The famous story about her is that Brochwel Ysgythrog, prince of Powys, was hunting a hare but lost his prey. He found the animal hiding under the dress of Melangell, who was praying amongst the brushwood. In spite of the urging of the prince, the hounds retreated from the woman. Brochwel confirmed the claim of the saint to her cell and lands and declared the site a refuge and sanctuary for man and animal forever.

Melangell became patron saint of hares and animals in general.

JUNE

5   Tudno – Confessor

It is said he was a son of Seithenyn, king of Cantre'r Gwaelod, whose lands were submerged 'through the wasteful neglect of the sentinel on the tower'. After this tragedy, Tudno and his brother became monks in the monastery of Bangor-on-Dee. The Nobility of the Saints associates him with Cyngreawdr, which is the Great Orme by Llandudno.

13   Dogfael – Confessor

In the *Progenies Keredig,* which is the lineage of Ceredig, there is a section

'Dogmael Sanctus, filius Ithaeil, filii Keredig' thus making this saint be related to the same line as David. Judging from the churches which bear his name, he lived and was a missionary in Pembrokeshire. In his ode to Saint Tydecho, Dafydd Llwyd of Mathafarn says that that saint was in St. Dogmael's with Dogfael, a legend which suggests that Dogfael and his monastery were famous and influential in his time.

29   Ceitho – Abbot, Confessor
One of the five saints commemorated in Llanpumsaint, in Carmarthenshire. His name is also to be found in Llangeitho. In the old calendars his feastday was August 5th.

JULY
1 Euddogwy – Bishop, Confessor
His life is contained in the Book of Llandaff. There it is said that he was the third bishop of that see, following Dyfrig and Teilo. Doble held that the author of the Book of Llandaff faked everything about Euddogwy. What he had done, according to Doble, was to take the name of bishop Eudoce, named in the life of Cadog, and identify him with the saint whose only commemoration is Llandogo, on the River Wye in Monmouthshire. Doble does not doubt the existence of a bishop called Eudoce in Glamorgan towards the end of the ninth century.

There was probably a famous monastery in Llandogo since the age of saints of the sixth century and this saint was held in high esteem in that area on the banks of the Wye.

According to the list in the Book of Llandaff, the first three bishops of the diocese were Dyfrig, Teilo and Euddogwy, and three of them together with Peter the Apostle were the patrons of the cathedral. It was to them the majestic church built by Urban in the twenties of the twelfth century was dedicated.

1   Julius and Aaron – Martyrs
Together with Alban, Julius and Aaron are the first martyrs of the Island of Britain. Gildas relates their experiences during the Diocletian persecution (303-313) saying 'rather than let Britain sink into the utter blackness of the dark night, (God) in his grace kindled the bright fire of the holy martyrs ... I speak of Alban of Verolanium and Julius and Aaron citizens of Caerleon'. (See: Gildas *De Excidio* 10, pp. 24-26.)

It is said Aaron's chapel was situated by the Roman camp on the River Usk.

To this day, the feastday of the two martyrs is kept in the calendar of the churches in Wales. In the calendar of the Catholic dioceses of the country, their feast is kept on June 20th.

17   Cynllo – King, Confessor
In some copies of the *Lineages of the Saints,* it is said that Cynllo was a brother of Teilo. He is associated mainly with north Radnorshire and he is patron of two churches in Ceredigion.

28   Samson – Abbot, Bishop, Confessor
Of all the lives of Welsh saints, the oldest by a long way to have survived is the *Vita Samsonis.* It was composed in Dol in Brittany at the beginning of the seventh century. According to the life, his mother brought the youthful Samson to the esteemed teacher Illtud and offered 'the usual gifts on such occasions'. Samson was a promising pupil and saintly. He was ordained a deacon in Llantwit Major by bishop Dyfrig and subsequently a priest by the same bishop. Soon afterwards, in order to retreat from the busy life of Illtud's school, Samson moved to Caldey Island. Against his will, he was appointed abbot and consecrated a bishop on the feast of Peter's Chair, February 22nd. It is not recorded which abbey he presided over, but it is assumed it was Llantwit Major. That place and Caldey are the only Welsh places associated with his name in the lives. The life says the monastery was established by Germanus. Tradition associates Illtud with Germanus and it is said that it was the saint from Auxerre who ordained Illtud a priest.

The fact that so many saints from south Wales are commemorated in Brittany testifies to the pastoral work and enthusiastic evangelising of the Welsh monks in their missions in the north of that peninsula.

Samson was a contemporary of David's and Teilo's. But, unlike the other two, his missionary activity was in Brittany. In Wales itself, he is mainly remembered in Caldey. The story about Teilo visiting him in Brittany to avoid the yellow plague suggests that Samson was a bishop there about the middle of the sixth century.

AUGUST
2   Garmon/Germanus – Bishop, Confessor
He was a bishop in Auxerre in France. According to Prosper of Aquitaine (c.390-463), a monk and contemporary of his, Germanus was sent to Britain in 429 by Pope Celestine I (September 422-July 432). He had been chosen by a synod in Gaul, together with Lupus, the bishop of Troyes, to delete the Pelagian heresy from the life of the Church in Britain. It is said he also returned again to Britain.

Within a half century to the period of Germanus, a life of him was composed by Constantius from Lyons. The life tells of his education as a lawyer, his career as a provincial administrator, and his selection by the popular voice as bishop of Auxerre. The picture we get from Constantius is of a bishop who lived a life of severe self-denial, and a renowned and highly respected church leader in his day. He died in Ravenna sometime between 437 and 448.

23 Tudful – Virgin, Martyr
One of Brychan's daughters named in *Cognacio Brychan,* a manuscript in the hand of Sir John Price, Brecon (c.1502-1555). Wade-Evans says the text which was copied came from the thirteenth century. It is said Merthyr Tydfil is named after her.

Iolo Morgannwg tells a story about her being killed as she visited her father in his old age in the place which still bears her name. We cannot be sure that this is a genuine tradition, and there was no feastday for her in the old calendars.

SEPTEMBER
5 Marchell – Queen
She was the mother of Brychan according to the lineages published in the VSBG. However, all that is there is mythical. We are told that Marchell, daughter of a British king called Tewdrig, sent her to Ireland to escape the lethal coldness. There she married King Anlach and gave birth to Brychan. She returned to Wales with her husband where Brychan was fostered.

Whatever the basis of this fable, it maintains the memory of a Christian mission in Breconshire and south-east Wales and of the close connection with Ireland.

11 Deiniol – Abbot, Bishop, Confessor
The tradition in the lives of the saints is that Deiniol was consecrated Bishop of Bangor by Dyfrig. In his lineage he is a son of Dunawd, son of Pabo Post Prydyn from the royal house of Rheged. He was a contemporary of Maelgwn Gwynedd. This is the period of Cybi and Cadfan and the most famous saints of Gwynedd. The suggestion in the lineages is that it was after the death of Maelgwn in 547 that the monastic revival in Gwynedd-is-Conwy started. The influence of the new movement had already extended in Uwch-Conwy. Bangor in Arfon was Deiniol's first establishment

Though there are rather few churches which bear his name, it can be said with confidence that the memory about him and devotion to him was common along the north, especially in Gwynedd. Churches were dedicated to him in Brittany also. This suggests that his relics had been taken there though it is possible he went there as a missionary for a while. It is quite probable that the tradition about him attending the Synod of Llanddewibrefi is genuine. According to the *Annales Cambriae,* he died in 584.

OCTOBER

1   Silin – Abbot, Confessor
Since the days of Iolo Morgannwg, at least, two different saints have been mixed up. One of them is Sulien who was said to come from Brittany towards the end of the sixth century. Apart from Iolo's manuscripts, his name appears in other calendars which give different dates for his feastday.

Silin is the Welsh form of the name of the abbot Giles who was such a popular saint in Britain. It is believed he was born in Greece and migrated to France. His feast was kept in England and Scotland since the eleventh century and on September 1st. In Wales, a church was dedicated to him in Wrexham. He is the saint commemorated in the name Llansilin, and is patron of churches in Pembrokeshire and Glamorgan. His feastday was kept on the first of September and the first of October in Wales.

5   Cynhafal – Confessor
We know nothing about this saint. The only church to bear his name is Llangynhafal in the Vale of Clwyd. It was believed that water from a well near the church was efficacious in curing warts and other body ailments.

9   Cynog – Bishop, Confessor
According to Giraldus Cambrensis, Cynog was Padarn's successor. He moved to fill the see of Menevia on the death of David. *The Annales Cambriae* say he died in 606.

The episcopal see of Ceredigion was Llanbadarn Fawr. The southern part of the county was part of the David's parrochia and the diocese of Menevia. Llanbadarn would have included parts of Breconshire, Radnorshire and, at times, parts of Montgomeryshire. It became part of the Menevia diocese in the eighth century.

The name of the saint is kept in Llangynog and in the names of parishes in Carmarthenshire, Breconshire and Montgomeryshire. There is no date for his feastday in the old calendars.

24   Crallo – Confessor
The name is preserved in Llangrallo (Coychurch) near Bridgend. The only details about him are to be found in Iolo Morgannwg's manuscripts. Edward Lluyd says that one of the springs near the church was called

Ffynnon Grallo (Crallo's Well).

NOVEMBER

2   Aelhaearn – Confessor
A saint from the seventh century and a brother to the saints Llwchaearn and Cynhaearn. There are churches dedicated to him in Powys, in Llanaelhaearn in Meirioneth and in the place with the same name near Tre'r Ceiri in Arfon. He was a disciple of Beuno's.

3   Gwenfrewi/Winifred – Virgin, Martyr
She flourished in the early years of the seventh century. According to the life, she was a daughter of a prince in Englefield and her mother was Gwenlo, a sister of St. Beuno. Caradog, prince of Hawarden cut her head off for rejecting his sexual advances. Beuno came from his church, lifted the head and restored it to the body. He prayed over her and resurrected her from the dead. Where the head had landed a well sprang up.

She spent the rest of her days in Gwytherin in Denbighshire where she was buried.

Up to the end of the fourteenth century, she was venerated in north Wales and the Marches and in Ewyas and Archenfield, two areas given to Herefordshire by Henry VIII. This supports the tradition that she spent time in Bodfari and in Henllan before moving to the monastery of Eleri in Gwytherin.

In 1138, her relics were moved to the Benedictine Abbey in Shrewsbury. This explains the devotion to her in the Marches. In 1398, Archbishop Roger Walden decreed that her feastday was to be kept throughout the province of Canterbury. In 1408, Archbishop Chichele, who was at the time bishop of St. David's, decreed that the feasts of David, Winifred and Chad should be kept in his province *cum regimine chori*, namely to be feast of the first order.

The pilgrimage to Winifred's sanctuary is the only one in Wales which has remained a popular one till this day. Because of the faithfulness of the Mostyn family of Talacre to the Old Faith, Holywell developed into the main centre of Catholic recusancy in north Wales, and remained a place of pilgrimage throughout all the years of persecution. The chapel and sanctuary were built by the mother of Henry VII after the Battle of Bosworth.

In the end of the seventeenth century, Edward Lluyd or one of his colleagues drew a sketch which he describes as 'Winifred's coffin in the church of Gwytherin in Denbighshire.' This sketch was discovered in the Bodleyan Library in Oxford, and a photograph of it and discussion about it were published in The Antiquaries Journal in 1990. It was suspected that the 'coffin' finally disappeared when the old church of Gwytherin was demolished in 1867. Strangely enough, Tristan Gray Hulse found a piece of wood in the Catholic presbytery in Holywell, wrapped in brown paper on which was written 'From the wooden chest at Gwytherin supposed to have contained the body of Winifred'. A discussion about the piece of wood by Nancy Edwards and Tristan Gray Hulse, was published, again, in The Antiquaries Journal in 1992.They demonstrate that the old wooden relic in Gwytherin was not Winifred's coffin but an old reliquary similar to those kept in Siena and Bologna in Italy. In 1997, Mr Gray Hulse found a fragment from the same reliquary.

6   Illtud – Abbot, Confessor
A saint and a key figure in the development of the Welsh nation. He is associated with Germanus and thus with the persistence of orthodox Christianity in Britain after the departure of the Roman legions. He was the teacher and spiritual father of the sixth century saints. It is fairly certain that he lived between 475 and 525. In the period of peace and tranquillity following the Battle of Mons Badonis, he was at it in Llantwit Major setting the foundations of learning and Christian life in Wales. Here and in Christian Ireland much of the intellectual and literary riches of Rome were treasured and re-introduced to continental Europe by the wandering monks of the succeeding centuries.

The old churches which bear Illtud's name are all in the south-east, in Breconshire, south Glamorgan and the Gower peninsula. The church of Llanelltud in Merioneth is dedicated to him as are the ancient churches of Leon, Treguier and Vannes in Brittany.

7   Cybi – Abbot, Confessor
According to the lives, he was the son of a leader of the king's retinue *(princeps militiae)* from Cornwall. His period is the middle of the sixth century. His main monastery was in Caergybi, namely Holyhead, where he lived within the walls of an old Roman fort. The cloister founded by him lasted till the sixteenth century.

According to the lives, Cybi received his education and monastic formation in his native district. Then he went on a pilgrimage to Jerusalem and to St. Hilary of Poitiers. He stayed in Gaul for over half a century and was ordained a bishop by Hilary. This is historically impossible because Hilary was bishop of Poitiers during the fourth century. But once again the connection with Gaul points to the trail of the monastic movement from Egypt through Italy and France to the Island of Britain.

A tradition was maintained in Anglesey that Cybi and Seiriol, abbot of Penmon, travelled regularly to meet in the parish of Llandyfrydog in order to discuss matters holy and spiritual. Cybi, walking eastwards in the morning and westwards in the evening as he returned to his monastery, always had his face to the sun whilst Seiriol had his back to it. Because of this Cybi had become tanned, and Seiriol retained his natural pallor. Thus they were called Cybi Felyn and Seiriol Wyn!

In the Welsh calendars, Cybi's feast was kept on November 5th, but the 7th and 8th are noted also.

8   Tysilio – Abbot, Confessor

A seventh century saint whose lineage is to be found in the *Nobility of the Saints*. He was said to be the son of Brochfael, the most famous hero in the old royal line of the princes of Powys. There is no life of him but in the ode by Cynddelw Brydydd Mawr, *Canu Tysilio Sant*, (The Song of Saint Tysilio), his mother is named as Garddun Benasgell. He is *'Tysilio ffyrnig ei filwriaeth'* (Tysilio, fierce in warfare), who 'won heaven in the districts of Eifionydd'. The poet says he went to Gwyddfarch, the patron saint of Meifod. This was the principal church of Meirioneth, burial place of kings, according to Cynddelw. As a monk, Tysilio held rich land on the isle of Sulio on the banks of the Menai Straits. According to the traditions recorded in Brittany in the fifteenth century, Tysilio had gone over there and built a church or churches. There is no historic basis for these traditions and it seems very unlikely he ever went on a mission to Brittany.

There are churches dedicated to him along the Menai Straits, in Meifod and in south Ceredigion and on the borders of Pembrokeshire and Carmarthenshire. E.G. Bowen said there was a fairly definite suggestion that he had travelled by sea along the coasts and evangelised in the nearby areas and in the estuaries of the rivers.

The tradition in Brittany is that Tysilio went there because of persecution by Hearted, widow of his brothers, because he had refused to turn his back on his monastic vows and marry her. It was because he wished to avoid loss and suffering to the church that he left his monastery in Anglesey. Cynddelw refers to this tradition.

12   Cadwaladr – King, Confessor

A prince and son of Cadwallon ap Cadfan. When his father was killed in 633, Gwynedd was taken over by the adventurer Cadfael ap Cynddelw. Cadwaladr did not receive his inheritance till 664.

He is remembered as Blessed Cadwaladr, patron saint of Llangadwaladr in Anglesey. Churches were dedicated to him in Denbigh and in Gwent. Henry Tudor traced his ancestry back to Cadwaladr, and Cadwaladr's red dragon was one of the three banners he presented to St. Paul's church in London after the Battle of Bosworth. He had probably heard about the prophecy of Geoffrey of Monmouth that Cadwaladr would return and the Britons would have 'their lordship of the island of Britain and their old merits' restored.

13   Dyfrig – Bishop, Confessor
He is the saint who somehow links the Christianity of the Roman period in Britain and the monastic revival in the sixth century. The life of him in the Book of Llandaff says he was of royal lineage. He became a famed Christian scholar and founded a monastery in Henllan (namely Hentland-on-Wye) where he taught pupils from near and far for seven years. Then he moved to his second foundation in Mochros or Moccas, where he stayed for a long period.

One of the great contributions of the Celtic Church was to accept that all branches of knowledge, Scriptural, theological, philosophical and literary tell us of God the Creator. It was not the intention of Dyfrig and his followers to develop scholars, what was important for them was to instruct Christians and clerics as a means of preserving all the Roman inheritance for the future, and it would all become one splendid whole in the Christian revelation.

Dyfrig was the bishop who ordained in Illtud's monastery. The Life talks of Pope Dyfrig arriving. By the early decades of the third century, the title 'pope' was used to denote a bishop. It was in the sixth century in the West that the title began to be reserved for the bishop of Rome, following the custom of the Imperial court in Constantinople in this matter. It was bishop Dyfrig who ordained deacons, priests and bishops.

The tradition is careful to maintain his right and privilege claiming that he had a ecclesiastical lineage through Germanus. It is unlikely that he was ordained bishop by Germanus, but it was Dyfrig who had secured and defended the orthodoxy and faithfulness of the Christians of Britain in a critical period. According to the Life, it was Dyfrig who consecrated the bishops of southern Britain and appointed Deiniol as bishop of Bangor. This emphasis on the relationship between Germanus and Dyfrig exists in all the major churches of Britain, and the further assertion that the wise men and learned men of Britain swarmed to Dyfrig's monastery encapsulates the tradition that the abbot-bishop Dyfrig had a role and special importance in the persistence of the true Christianity of Wales and Roman Britain.

Dyfrig is also associated with Caldey island, where, according to the Life of Samson, he would spend Lent. According to the testimony of that life, Dyfrig was highly respected and the memory of him very alive and influential in Llantwit and Caldey.

As an old man it is said he retired from his laborious work and retreated to Bardsey Island, where he died and was buried amongst the multitude of saints.

He was not allowed to rest there, however, to await the resurrection of the dead. In 1120, bishop Urban of Llandaff and his clerics went up to Gwynedd. Urban was the first to call himself bishop of Llandaff and claim Dyfrig and Teilo as his predecessors. He already had Teilo's body in Llandaff cathedral, but that was only one out of three, and Llandeilo Fawr and Tenby also claimed they had Teilo's body. Even Urban did not dare deny that Teilo had been buried in Llandeilo. Therefore he felt he had to get hold of Dyfrig's body for Llandaff. In co-operation with the prince of Gwynedd and the bishop of Bangor, Urban went at it to dig on Bardsey. Early in May he found Dyfrig's bones and they were borne, together with the arm of Elgar, an English hermit, to Llandaff. It had been an extraordinarily dry spring, and on the Sunday, May 23rd, Dyfrig's body was received into Llandaff cathedral. There was much rejoicing and amazement amongst the natives as they saw clouds gathering and pouring rain on the land and earth of the area. The saint, was seen to be blessing his new home as his bones were laid in their final resting place. Urban decided to build a majestic and splendid church that would be worthy of the saints which were henceforth to rest in Llandaff.

According to Wade-Evans, Dyfrig died in 556. That date is too late. In the *Dictionary of Welsh Biography*, Hywel D. Emanuel suggests 475 as the time of his work and influence.

25   Paulinus – Bishop, Confessor

The Life of Paul, whose surname is given as Aurelius, was written in Landevennec monastery in Brittany. The author is Wrmonoc and he says he finished the work in 884. It is quite unusual to be able to date the composition of the lives of the early saints. The surname Aurelius recalls the British prince Ambrosius Aurelianus, Emrys Wledig in the Welsh tradition, the hero of the battles against the Saxon tribes in the second half of the fifth century and who was killed during them.

In the life we hear that he was a son of a chieftain called Perphirius and that he was born in Penychen in south-east Glamorgan. Also, that Paul and his brothers lived in Brehant Dincat. G.H.Doble argues that that place is Llandovery.

Wrmonoc goes on to say that Paul was sent as a youth to Illtud's school where he was a contemporary of David, Gildas and Samson. This is in contradistinction to what Rhigyfarch says about David, newly ordained as a priest, going to Paulinus, the disciple of Germanus, and that David restored the sight of his master who had gone blind. Paulinus was also one of the bishops who counselled inviting David to the Synod of Llanddewibrefi. It is quite possible that the confusion was between two different saints. The opening of Wrmonoc's Life suggests this as he first mentions Benychen before moving without warning to a family living in Brehant Dincat. And certainly there has been much confusion in the Middle Ages between Paulinus the Welshman and the other Paulinus who was bishop of York, and who died in 644.

Wrmonoc is writing about the saint who gave his name to the little city of St.-Pol-de-Leon in Brittany. He says that Paul or Paulinus left Llanddeusant at the request of Marc, king of Cornwall, and settled in a place called Caer Banhed. Soon afterwards he moved to his sister in Brittany.

As we try to interpret all the traditions, I think it possible to suggest that there was a saint called Paul or Paulinus who flourished during the generation before David and Teilo. He is connected, amongst others, with these two which suggests that he was saint from the south. If so, then Illtud's school was not the only centre of learning in the south nor the only nursery of saints. He can, with Illtud, be called a teacher and instructor of saints.

DECEMBER
1   *Tudwal – Bishop, Confessor*
A saint who is commemorated in Brittany and Wales. His name is not mentioned amongst the saints in the old lineages. His ancestry is written about by Iolo Morgannwg. It is obvious that Iolo has confused the lineage of the leader of the Britanni with the other Tudwal who has three lives composed about him, which were written in Brittany.

Saint Tudwal is associated with the emigration from Cornwall to Brittany. He came of a royal line. In the lives as in the Matins homilies, all the saints were either of noble birth or a poor but honest family. When Tudwal got to Brittany Paul had already established his monastery in Leon. Tudwal, therefore, went on to Treguier and built a large monastery there.

There are two islands on the east coast of the Llŷn peninsula which bear Tudwal's name. On the larger of the two, the eastern one, there was a chapel in the Medieval period dedicated to the saint. The chapel was turned into a haybarn. Then, in 1886, the island was bought by a Welsh Catholic priest, Henry Bailey Hughes, with the intention of establishing a monastery there. His plan was to bring young men from Brittany to start a mission to the local populace of Aber-soch and Llŷn. After a year of hard living on the island and in Llŷn he died on December 16th, 1897. The little community was dispersed and the Bretons returned to their own country.

4   Cawrdaf – King, Confessor

His feast is held on this day according to the old Welsh calendars. Iolo Morgannwg, seeing this, elevated him to be a bishop.

The few traditions we have about Cawrdaf suggest that he belonged to the seventh century. His name is connected with Aber-soch in Gwynedd, and it is there his image was kept, his book and holy bell.

18   Tydecho – Abbot, Confessor

With the exception of the ode to Saint Tydecho by Dafydd Llwyd of Mathafarn, there is no life of this saint. According to tradition he was a brother of Samson's. He is mentioned in the Life of Padarn where it is said he was one of three leaders of groups of saints who came over from Brittany. There was a deal of traffic across the sea between Wales and the other Christian countries, especially between the Celtic countries. The churches which bear the names of saints who were said to have come from Brittany to Wales are almost all in the river valleys which run into Cardigan Bay. Tydecho is mostly commemorated in Cwm Mawddwy. He is the patron of Llan-ym-Mawddwy and the nearby parishes, Cemais, Garthbeibio and Mallwyd. Here are the opening words of Dafydd Llwyd's ode:

Mae gŵr llwyd yma gerllaw
Mawl a wedd yn aml iddaw;
Crefyddwr cryf o Fawddwy,
Ceidwad eu hollwlad hwy;
Tydecho lwys, tad uwchlaw,
Un o filwyr nef aelaw.

(There is a pale man nearby
Who deserves praise often;
A strong religious man from Mawddwy,
Keeper of all its land;
Comely Tydecho, father above,
One of abundant heaven's soldiers.)

According to the ode, he was a hermit with his sister Tegfedd. He was troubled by Maelgwn Gwynedd. He was said to have been 'grandson of Emyr the Breton who then migrated to Mawddwy'.

He was a saint of the sixth century, and it is said that the water of Tydecho's Well in Garthbeibio was good for arthritis.

He appears under the Latin form Tatheus in the Life of Tathan published in VSBG by Wade-Evans. As there is a reference there to the bishop of Llandaff, the present text cannot be older than the period of Urban, the first to use that name. The title of bishops in south-east Wales prior to Urban was Teilo's Bishop.

The life tells us that Tathan was born in Ireland, son of king Tuathal. That king about whom there is definite evidence belonged to the sixth century. On the other hand, it is said Tathen was a teacher of Cadog's. If this were true, it would place him fairly certainly in the fifth century. Tathan settled in Gwent and received his lands from the king there in order to found the monastery of Caer-went. By the fifth century this Roman town was one of the strongest centres of Christianity in this part of Britain. By Tathan's time, the battle to stop the Saxon raids into the West had commenced.

Because of the name of the village in the Vale of Glamorgan, Sain Tathan (St. Athan's), Iolo Morgannwg devised a story to connect Tathan with it in an honourable way. Unfortunately, in older documents, we hear of eccelesia Tathane. The patron of the village in the Vale of Glamorgan is an unknown saint.

Bibliography

A substantial number of specialist studies on the early saints and on the Church in the Celtic countries have been published in specialist journals and periodicals. A list of there would be rather long. I limit this short bibliography to the books which are easy to get hold of. Though some of these books have been out of print for years, they are available in our public libraries.

S.Baring-Gould and John Fisher: *The Lives of the British Saints: Volumes 1 to 4*, London 1907-1913.

A.W. Wade-Evans: *Vitae Sanctorum Britannia et Genealogiae;* Cardiff 1944.

J. Gwenogryn Evans, John Rhys: *The Text of the Book of Llan Dav*, Oxford 1903.

A.W. Wade-Evans: *The Emergence of England and Wales*, Cambridge 1956, 1959.

G.H. Doble: (D. Simon Evans ed.) *Lives of the Welsh Saints*, Cardiff 1971.

N.K. Chadwick (ed.) *Studies in the Early British Church*, Cambridge 1958.

Francis Jones: *The Holy Wells of Wales*, Cardiff 1992.

E.G. Bowen: *The Settlements of the Celtic Saints in Wales*, Cardiff 1954.

E.G. Bowen: *Saints, Seaways and Settlements in Celtic Lands*, Cardiff 1967, 1977.

D. Simon Evans: *Buchedd Dewi*, Cardiff 1959.

D. Simon Evans: *The Welsh Life of St David*, Cardiff 1988.

Dom Louis Gougaud: *Christianity in Celtic Lands*, London 1932.

Molly Miller: *The Saints of Gwynedd*, Cambridge 1979.

R.P.C. Hanson: *St Patrick: His Origins and Career*, Oxford 1968.

L. Bieler: *The Life and Legend of St Patrick*, Dublin 1948.

D.R. Howlett: *The Book of Letters of St Patrick The Bishop*, Dublin 1994.

Elissa R. Henken: *Traditions of the Welsh Saints*, Cambridge 1987.

Silas M.Harris: *St David in the Liturgy*, Cardiff 1940.

Owain Tudor Edwards: *Matins, Lauds and Vespers for St David's Day*, Cambridge.

Charles Thomas: *Britain and Ireland in Early Christian Times*, London 1971.